T0365625

WORTHY TREASURES

Part II – Journeys in Panarico[1]

iUniverse books may be ordered through booksellers or by contacting:

iUniverse
1663 Liberty Drive
Bloomington, IN 47403
www.iuniverse.com
844-349-9409

Because of the dynamic nature of the Internet, any web addresses or links contained in this book may have changed since publication and may no longer be valid. The views expressed in this work are solely those of the author and do not necessarily reflect the views of the publisher, and the publisher hereby disclaims any responsibility for them.

Any people depicted in stock imagery provided by Getty Images are models, and such images are being used for illustrative purposes only. Certain stock imagery © Getty Images.

All rights reserved on photos and literary works.

ISBN: 978-1-6632-5619-5 (sc)
ISBN: 978-1-6632-5620-1 (hc)
ISBN: 978-1-6632-5618-8 (e)

Library of Congress Control Number: 2023917341

Print information available on the last page.

iUniverse rev. date: 09/29/2023

WORTHY TREASURES

Part II – Journeys in Panarico

By
Judy Reyes-Maggio
&
James Reyes

Dedication

•───●─•

Judy Reyes-Maggio, the Panarican Poetess[2]

Dedicated to my mom for 53 years and 8 months of unconditional love, and my dad for 7 years of unconditional love.

James Reyes, the Panarican Poet[3]

Dedicated to my family and friends for all their support and love keeping me on my journey and being there.

I also dedicate this work to those who deal with Parkinson's. May we see the cure someday soon!

Contents

Section 1

More Dreams

By
Judy Reyes-Maggio
The Panarican Poetess

Quote

• ● •

Today's decisions become tomorrow's past and
future. Always do what is right based on what you
know and believe. There is no time for regrets.

Judy Reyes-Maggio

Photo of framed Panamanian Mola (hand-made art form) of
Panamanian macaws, owned by JR-M 2023

The Sprinter Jean
(excerpts 2022)

How many of you have had an epiphany? For me, it is like a twister of thoughts swirling in my head. Then, there is a light…. then, "I can see clearly now, the fog is gone…"

I knew it! You are having an epiphany right now. You are absolutely right – I am the backup singer for the group, the Howling Hounds. [HOWL for 3 seconds….]

In March of this year, my younger sister said to me, "Hey Judy, did you know I have the sprinter gene? Who would have thought, I have never been able to use it." I was befuddled, "Did mom make you a sprinter jean too?" My sister looked at me, befuddled, "WHAT?!" I said, "Did mom make you a sprinter jean? Don't you remember how mom would say all the time that I sprinted everywhere? That in order to keep me from wearing down my clothes, she made me a sprinter jean. Yes, a sprinter jean… and I still have it."

My sister was silent for a moment and then said, "Judy, I am talking about the sprinter gene, GENE, not JEAN. My DNA analysis says I have the sprinter gene, GENE." My jaw dropped wide open "Huh, you have the sprinter gene, the same sprinter gene that Usain Bolt of Jamaica, Allison Felix of the USA, Karsten Warholm of Norway, and Susana Kallur of Sweden have???" Quietly my sister said "Yes."

Memories swirled in my head…..my epiphany had begun…..

At 4 years of age, I deliberately broke the porcelain top of the toilet tank in the powder room. My mom ran out of the kitchen, screaming, "Judy, I am going to get you, you little buggar." With my sprinter jean on, I outran my mother up two flights of stairs. Yes, I ran like a chicken, fast and fearful…..I was not going to get spanked.

At 7 years of age, on the playground at recess, I was challenged to a fight. I offered an alternative, a race from home plate to second base, and back. If I won, there would be no fights, ever. Of course I had my sprinter jean on, I flew like the wind, and won. No need for scratches or bruises, and my pretty face was intact.

At 9 years of age, my family was enjoying a rare fishing day at one of the lakes near Fort Gordon, Georgia. My sister and I were watching my 10- month baby brother who walked very wobblily. In the blink of an eye, he was out in the middle of the dirt road that passed by the lake. My sister and I were horrified when we saw a car slowly plowing towards my baby brother. Yes, I was wearing my sprinter jean and I took off…. picked him up in my arms, jumped and flew throw the air, landing on the other side of the road. As the car passed us by, the driver was screaming, "She is faster than a speeding bullet. It's Supergal!" At the same time my sister, who was standing on the other side of road screamed, "Mami, a car almost hit the baby…"

In high school, I played in the powder puff match between juniors and seniors. I was a running back or halfback for the senior team. Can you hear it, I can hear it, the chant in the stands every time I carried the football, oh, yes: "Floating like a butterfly, flying like bee, that girl there will dash by thee." The school and local papers wrote, "The seniors' secret weapon, Judy in her sprinter jean, sped down the field, like a lightning bolt, touchdown after touchdown."

In my combo junior-senior year, I was part of the university's first women's track and field team. It's a given - I always wore my sprinter jean. I held the records for the 200, 400, and 800 meters, for a grand total of 1 year!!

I am seeing the light…I can see clearly now the fog is gone…[Howl for 3 seconds]

I know you just had the same epiphany I did ..you are absolutely right – in addition to the sprinter JEAN that my mami made for me, my DNA analysis shows I, have the sprinter GENE.

Simple Stories
(excerpts 2021)

In elementary school, I raided the classroom library. Reading biographies was exciting. Madame Curie, a physicist who conducted pioneer research on radioactivity and the first woman to win the Nobel Prize. Amelia Earhart, the first woman to fly solo across the Atlantic Ocean. I was so impressed, I named my first pet, my very own first pet, an Eastern box turtle, Amelia Earhart.

Once upon a time, there was an 8 year old girl, who stood 3 feet tall with thick straight ebony hair down to her knees. Standing on the slopes of the volcanic crater her family called home for thousands of years, she stared at the mountain range named (in her native language) "La india dormida." The sun star was bright, not a cloud in the sky, as she peered out through the lush rainforest. Her tiny left hand cradled over her eyes while she held a machete in her right. Fearlessly, she listened to the sounds of the jungle: the trickling crystalline waterfalls, the roars of the jaguars and cougars, and the slithering of venomous snakes. She dreamed of a life far beyond the volcanic crater.

Twenty-two years passed, and she found herself in a different land, a different culture, where she did not speak the language. As her six children grew up in this new culture, she would tell them simple stories of life. One day, she told a simple story. "My dear child, I never had the chance to complete my schooling. When I was 8, my teacher came to our ranch. Even though in my country, it was unheard of for an indigenous person to be anything but a laborer or a maid, she believed I had the potential to become a teacher. She asked my parents to allow me to be part of a special program. But my parents needed me to help in the fields, and said no. Now, my dream is for you. I want you to receive the education I never received and achieve what I cannot achieve."

All six of her children went to college with athletic or academic scholarships, full or part-time work, student loans, and the Pell grant. Three children studied accounting. One of the three had a master's in business administration. Another of the three had a dual degree in computer programming as well as being a Certified Public Accountant, and a Certified Information Systems Auditor. A fourth child became a licensed pharmacist while another studied biology and a master's in project management. Lastly, one child was an electrical engineer with two master's degrees, in electrical engineering and business administration. Four of her children were high level executives: 2 in the private sector and 2 in the federal sector.

A simple story about an impossible dream that seemed so unreachable is my mother's legacy.

Reading the stories about Madame Curie and Amelia Earhart was inspirational. But my mother is my greatest inspiration.

"Mi Mami Me Decía"
(2009)

Mi mami me decía

Que un día no iba estar.

Cuando yo pensaba en ese día

Mi corazón no dejaba de llorar.

Ponía mi cabecita sobre mis manos

Y me acostaba a dormir,

Y cuando me recordaba

Que mi mami me decía

Que un día no iba estar,

No dejaba de llorar.

Así fue toda mi vida

Desde kindergarten hasta

Hoy en día.

Cuando me acuerdo de me mami

No dejo de llorar.

Ella esta en el cielo

Y se que esta mejor que aquí.

Aun así,

Mi alma no deja de llorar.

Saved!
(2023)

Mom, you were always there for me.
Even though I did not understand it all -
I believed in you.
My high school counselor said that I could,
And should go to college in the states.
You believed in me, and I believed I would.
You took me to my first job interview
And assessed everyone there.
You did that all for me.
You helped me carry the typewriter
Into the Federal building for the test
That led me to my federal career.
You did that all for me.
When any one was unfair to me
You wanted to greet them at the door;
In order to protect me even more.

As far as I can remember you
You gave me words of wisdom.
Your words will always be with me,
In my soul, heart, and mind.
"Ten cuidado, no salgas de noche."
"No comas o bebes nada sin chequear."
"Siempre cierra las puertas.
Ten cuidado."
"Las drogas no son nada bueno."
"No seas pichicumba[4]."
"Ojo al pillo."
Seeing how much you loved me
Gave me strength every day.
In life, situations do arise.
Mom, your words are always there.
Countless are the times your
Words of wisdom saved me from regret.
Mom, you saved me!

MOM
(2009)

You gave us life.
You gave us love.

Loving us was your gift
That lies forever in our hearts.
We were there to see you leave--
We saw your last tear drop of love
As you entered God's heaven of peace.

We miss you every day,
And remember you in every way.

Me enseñaste lo grande del amor
Me enseñaste lo que es valor-
Me enseñaste verdad a pesar del dolor-
Esto y mucho más resuena en mi corazón.
Gracias mamita querida por ser mía.

Una Flor Eterna y Preciosa
(2021)

Mi mami, una flor eterna y preciosa.
Para mí, fuiste como la luna y mi sol.
Me enseñaste como amar,
En medio de alegría y dolor.
Con tus ejemplos, nos has encaminado,
En esta vida, en tu jardín bien cultivado.
Gracias mami, por tus palabras sabias,
Tu testimonio, tu rol de mama y papa.
Nunca estamos listos para verter ir.
Para verte llorar o sufrir.
Te echare de menos el resto de mi vida,
Escuchare tu voz en todo sonido,
Te veré en cada momento que traspire.
Mami, tu fragancia de flor hermosa
Siempre en mi corazón estará.

Photo of home grown flower by JR-M 2023

A Fresh Memory
(2022)

Every Christmas, I dream of mami-made rice and beans,
Oven-baked turkey stuffed with potatoes or rice,
with fried sweet slices of the
ripened plantains, the banana doppelganger,
Or the crunchie fried slices of green plantains.
Add slices of avocado and a ripe red tomato.
The appetizers, codfish stew or a vegetable medley
Soup of yuca, yautia, name, y guineitos.
In English, yucca, yautia, white yam, and tiny green bananas.
For dessert: arroz con dulce (rice pudding), flan (custard),
or tembleque (coconut trembling pudding).
Such a delicious a meal!
I also dream of lights inside and out,
the more the merrier,
The brighter the better.
We laugh, we play games, we open gifts,
And we are grateful for the time together.
For me, every Christmas is a fresh memory of my mami.
As Jose Feliciano sang,
"Feliz Navidad…..
We (want to) wish you a Merry Christmas."

Photo of home-made Christmas cake by JR-M 2018

Photo of ceramic Christmas tree owned by JR-M (2023). For years, a similar tree was displayed every Christmas by JR-M's mother.

Independence
(2022)

"I want to be free." The cry of many.
Thirteen colonies spoke out against tyranny.
Fought fiercely with much dreaded bloodshed.
And broke the chains of the crowned head.
"I want to be free." The cry of the poor.
Who stares at the cupboard, there is no more.
Studied hard and left hunger behind
For a land of wealth with little time.
"I want to be free." The cry of a wife.
Battered, stuck in a lonely life.
Silenced the crying, and the lying,
With love for God and her six scions.
"I want to be free." The cry of a baby.
Nine months in the womb of her beloved mami.
Born into a world of even more sorrow.
Even so, believed in a brighter tomorrow.
"I want to be free." The cry of a lonely man.
Gave up his children's love like a bad poker hand.
War hero, or not, with remorse was besot
Until in God's web he was finally caught.
Now, I, look at the times with much delight
And know that no matter the spite,
There is no doubt I am truly free,
Since the day Jesus came and saved me.

Photo of framed Puerto Rican artwork owned by JR-M 2023

El sombrero viejo
(2021)

———— ●—— ————

Cuarenta años pasaron, y no te reconocí
Si tu hubiese en mi camino cruzado,
Nunca pensaría que mi papi estaba a mi lado.
Los años te dejaron huellas en tu rostro,
Dejaron marcas profundas en tu alma,
Y tu mirada, muy adolorida estaba.

Como un sobrero viejo, que se ha usado,
Con sudor marcado y poco lavado.

Cuando nos vistes te asombraste
Al ver a tus hijas tan crecidas.
Mirabas con ansia a ver se podías
Captar lo profundo de nuestros corazones;
Si había, aunque pequeño, una morada,
A pesar de cuarenta años de estar aislados.

Como un sobrero viejo, que se ha usado,
Con sudor marcado y poco lavado.

Disfrutamos conocerte en esos días soleados,
En la Florida, en un pueblo muy poblado.
De tu hermana quisiste huir, y yo me recordaba,
"el judío errante" así mi mami te llamaba.
Nosotras muy contentas estábamos-
Pediste vernos de nuevo y visitarnos.

Como un sobrero viejo, que se ha usado,
Con sudor marcado y poco lavado.

Fue en un mes de abril que te buscamos,
Y nos llamabas para que no te olvidáramos.
Nos tomo un día llegar y un día regresar
Al estado de Virginia, a un pueblito muy americano.
En verdad, no te conocía; los pocos recuerdos
De ti estaban envueltos en dolor.

Como un sobrero viejo, que se ha usado,
Con sudor marcado y poco lavado.

Papi, todavía tengo tu sombrero viejo
El que usabas en esos días primeros.
También tengo todos tus regalos -

Todos los sombreros nuevos que usabas.
Y con ellos los recuerdos de un amor
De padre e hija eternamente dorado.

Photo of daddy's hat owned by JR-M 2023

Phases of the Moon
(excerpts 2023)

———— ●—●—● ————

I was five years old when I heard the nursery rhyme, "Hey Diddle Diddle, the cat and the fiddle, the cow jumped over the moon.." That last verse intrigued me. For many months, I propped my little head on my bedroom windowsill. The eight phases of the moon fascinated me as I waited for a cow to appear.

Ring. Ring.

"Hello."

"Judy, our father is looking for us. He lives in Miami with his sister."

""What does that have to do with me?"

"Do you want his phone number and address?"

"No." click.

I stood there shaking in emotional uncertainty. Forty years had passed since I had last seen my father. Never in a blue moon had I expected to hear from him.

My brother's phone call incited a battle between my mind, heart, and soul. What should I do? My mind and heart came to a truce, and my soul led the way.

Since my father had been brave enough to call my brother, I could be brave enough to call him. When I heard my father's voice, I was startled. Two weeks after we spoke, I flew to Miami to see him. At the airport, I walked past him. When we came face to face, and looked into each other's eyes, we were strangers.

My father came to live with my husband, my two elderly English Mastiffs, and me. He was about 81 and a half years old. He had a few pieces of clothing, and more than half of his prescriptions were expired. He was a quiet man. I sensed a lonely man. I decided to do what my husband and my sister say I do best, talk and ask questions.

My father joined the United States Army because he needed a job, but it was his calling. For a short period of time, he was part of the famed 65th Infantry Regiment. Later he was assigned to a group that dealt with missiles and protected Washington, DC. During the Cuban Missile Crisis, he was part of a secret mission to land on the beaches of Cuba. While training soldiers for the Vietnam War, his grenade launcher jammed. The grenade blew up before he could move away. He was in a coma for several months and not expected to live. He recovered and served three tours in Vietnam. In his first two tours, he fought on the front lines and on his last tour he was part of an intelligence group. He earned various commendations for valor. I realized my father was an incredible soldier, a decorated war hero, and forever a part of history.

My father was 2 years old when his mother died. His stepmother did not love him. He struggled with alcoholism and gambling since he was a teenager. His second marriage failed. His stepsons beat him in order to take his money. Many times he woke up lying in a ditch. Because of his disabilities, his older sister planned to place him in a nursing home. I understood that my father had never found happiness.

In the latter years, my Daddy slowed down. A pacemaker was implanted under the skin of his chest. His arthritis worsened. A caregiver accompanied him whenever I was not home. He fell down several times and sprained his ankles. I spent many nights caring for him.

One evening as I was cooking dinner, my Daddy came to the kitchen. Quietly, he said, "Judy, my hour has come." I hugged him and sweetly asked, "Daddy, I thought you were going to reach 90?" He shrugged his shoulders. Through my tears I told him how much I loved him, and what a blessing he was in our lives. We hugged, and he said, "Life is like the phases of the moon. I am entering another phase."

Early the next morning, I heard him calling my name. I found him lying on the bedroom floor. As I cradled him in my arms, my Daddy crossed over the pink moon.

When I heard the military gun salute at his funeral, I thought of the 2604 days or 7 years my Daddy was with me. Together, we lived the fullness of a lifetime. Forgiveness and love completed us.

Today, I am happy I had the best Dad ever. I was "Daddy's little girl."

Photo of pink moon by JR-M 2020

Soy Como la Luna
(2017)

"Soy como la luna,

estoy pasando por una fase."

Fueron las palabras de un hombre sabio

En sus últimos momentos de inspiración.

Pensando en su vida, como la paginas se habían escrito.

Entendía que se acababa la tinta de esta vida terrenal.

Y contemplando, dijo,

"Está llegando mi tiempo."

Se acercaba la primavera,

con sus flores y calor,

Cuando su ultimo capitulo en

esta vida efímera se escribió.

Pero entonces comenzó

la próxima fase de su cuento…

La fase de estar con su Señor,

¡En una vida eterna de resplandor!

Remembering 9/11/2001 (2021)

Some of you had not even been born, but here is a memory of 20 years ago today.

It was a regular workday. My younger disabled sister and I rode a bus to our jobs in downtown DC. She worked in an office one block from the White House. I worked in an office two blocks from the White House.

It was a typical morning for me - very, very busy, and I was there since 7 AM. All the executives were away at a Leadership retreat. Shortly after 8:00 am, I noticed that the Acting Director turned on the TV (used to show videos) in the executive conference room. Then at about 8:46 am, the Acting Director alerted us that a plane had crashed into the Twin Towers in NYC – I saw the replays on TV. At that point, we were waiting for further instructions from Headquarters as to what to do next. We kept trying to do some work.

At about 9:37 am, a plane crashed into the Pentagon. My sister called me to tell me she had been released from work, but my office had not been told to leave. I told her to walk to Farragut West Metro, and wait for me across the street, across from the office building where my youngest brother worked, and to call him. At about 9:50 am, my office was told to leave. I ran around the office making sure everyone was gone.

I looked out of my office window several times and saw a mob of people walking the streets – they looked like a swarm of ants walking aimlessly. I left my office building between 9:55 and 10 am.

I do not remember how long it took me to meet my sister, but it was around 10:20 am. While I was walking there, with hundreds of others, I overheard that the Farragut West metro was shut down. My sister called me and told me my youngest brother had been released from his office after the first plane crashed into the Twin Towers. The office building where he worked was right next to the White House. He had just arrived at his house.

What my sister and I did not know as we were walking and standing in the streets of DC was that Flight 93 had been hijacked. It is believed that if the heroes on Flight 93 had not rebelled against the hijackers and forced the plane to crash in Pennsylvania, Flight 93 would have crashed into either the White House or the Capitol between 10:13 and 10:22 am.

At 10:13 am, I was less than one block from the White House, and my sister was across the street from the White House. At 10:22 am, my sister and I were across the street from the White House. If Flight 93 had crashed into the White House, my sister and I would not be here today.

REFLECTION: GOD has a purpose for all of us. No matter what you are going through, look to GOD first. Be grateful for all that He has given you as our time on earth is defined. Do the best you can in everything, not because you want to be better, but because all your talents and abilities were given to you by GOD. Be good and do the right thing – help others to the best of your abilities.

A Baby Boy
(2022)

I remember I did not know why mami was getting fat.
One day our Panamanian aunties came to care for my sister and me…
Play was the name of game, and we tied them onto chairs.
We heard their cries while we played outside…
It was hot, it was clammy, it was Panama weather.
Mami came home with a baby boy.
His name was James – my Dad wanted Jaime-
But my mami said it had to be English.
Such tiny little hands and feet,
I kind of recall that he cried a lot.
By the time he was one, he was a special tot.
Smart, curious, and talkative indeed.
Both Mom and Dad looked at him in awe.

Family photo owned by JR-M

Section 2

Dreams Continue

By James Reyes

The Panarican Poet

"You can and should strive for accuracy

And precision. You may need a little more
Focus and concentration. Hit as many
Targets as you can…believe in yourself.
You do not want to give up anything.
In fact, I think you can live more by being

Focused and using time more wisely.
For me, it was a constant reminder that I
Have things to do and I need to get them done
While the sun still rises and shines
On me. Whatever happens….I have
gotten more than I ever thought I would
And every day, every experience is a bonus!"

VOLANDO ADELANTE

Dreams

Keep dreaming big.
As the biggest can come true
Stay true to yourself and
The best may happen.
To you

See the beauty all around
The stars in the skies
The horizon so far
See the sun rise.

Family and friends
They are the prize.
Look at the good all around
All through your eyes

From my perspective
The Stream never cries.

Keep DREAMING BIG!
And your dream never dies

Proponents of Support

As a mentor for minorities in my professional career I had the opportunity to help many people. I was awarded two diversity beacon awards, one for the company. I also won Hispanic leader role model of the year. As part of the acceptance ceremony, I had the opportunity to speak. One of the things I said was "someday the sun will rise on a day where everyone brings their best to the table and is recognized for their contributions and potential…"

I always dreamed grande!

Rice and Beans
With chopped onions

———— •—●—• ————

What would I like my family to know.

About my life.

How did I get here?

Because that has something to do with how they all are where they are.

My goal always was to be a positive influence.

My family: I wanted to provide a good environment for them to grow up in
and to be able to let go.

When they left the nest.

And be there for whatever they needed.

And hopefully to be included in their lives as well.

Life could be viewed as a continuum of ripe plantains and avocados.

You have to be very good at judging what is ripe. And when is the right time?

To serve it, cook it or fry it. Or whatever makes it delectable. That is true
of life as well. It is not always delectable. But you can always try to get
it back. To where you know it will be delectable.

My life has been a continuum of experiences. They were not necessarily all
good. And most of which I could learn from. But I have had probably more
than my fair share of what I would call positive to great experiences

And I think as an individual you have a lot to say and do
about how positive your life is.

So, like in any other... Analysis ...About life... You will see that...
Most Negative experiences? And everything in between.
My favorite subject was math, so. I'm going to take some license here.
And use a lot of analogies associated with me and my predilection for math.
So, in that vein, I am going to set up a geometric proof or the like just to be sure.
You know I succeeded in what I set out to do with my life. And that.
The goals I chose were not necessarily easy, but did I accomplish most of them?

Nonetheless. In short. I wanted to be a Good, if not great, father. Her
great husband. And the great grandfather? I also wanted to be successful in
life. So that we could be one of the first in our family that retired and left
something for the next generation. So, we'll have to use statistics to see
how we prove this. It sounds like it could be a wild ride.

I have to ask you. Are you up to that? Because every life is unique. And mine
is no different. But I'll have to continue to rely on those ripe plantains and
avocados. Because they are the right ripe fuel for this story?
(Or should it have been rice and beans)?

(rice & beans with French bread, NY strip & chateaubriand and pineapple soda)

Happy to continue...
(2020)

The proceedings continue.
The underdog is still trying.
The odds not so good
But there are still odds.

In the end there may not be victory
But I have already won.
I have gained so much.
From the lives I have touched

I must continue to go forward.
There is so much beauty to see.
I will be the big papi.
My grandson will see.

As long as I can
I plan to endure.
It does not get easier.
Of that much I am sure

Another day starts.
A cloudy sunrise
I contain my excitement.
It feels like a triple prize.

Purpose and the Ocean
(2023)

The bulk of my life I was clear of purpose and had many things to do... I was on the beach and could build almost anything if the sand was just right. I would have to modify or change the structure depending on the tide and where I was on the beach. Some creations were more permanent than others. I always was one to stay in the sand and get my feet wet and sometimes get my face wet too. I always felt in control and while I felt the pull of the undertow, I never thought about it too much. I realize now it was my youth and arrogance that made me feel in control of the ocean (especially if you are not a strong swimmer). Many of us lose some motivation as purpose changes and or wanes. In addition, our abilities may change. I am a little humbler now with 25 years of Parkinson's to realize that the truth of the matter is now the ocean is pulling and I am in the water doing what I can to tread water and sometimes make it to the beach and do something even if it is just to feel the sand one more time. The pull of the ocean is powerful. Yet serene and soothing. I could relax and let it take me, but I still feel very strongly I have purpose and need to do a few things. I do some days wake and wonder about who needs me or my purpose. I am being worn down by the endless supply of waves taking their toll. As confident as I was, I have begun to feel doubt as do I really have further purpose and does anyone really need me. The undertow is pulling. The ocean is powerful. But I still dream and find more to be done. This beach is not crowded anymore...is that a sunset beginning? In my case, I am either too strong willed or too stubborn to give in or give up or surrender. The day may come. But hopefully not soon. There is still so much I want to see and do. I think we should all be aware if and when our feelings or sense of purpose changes or fluctuates. This flag is the vehicle that allows us to help ourselves or get help.

While sunsets are beautiful, I am more interested in the sunrise, because that is a new day, to wake up, dream and do! It is still my routine.

I wonder...

If your purpose is very true.
It very well may fall on you.
If your big dreams drive you fore
Coming true, may be your lore

Look east for the next sunrise
Your purpose you must reprise
It can fill us with new hope
And more ability to cope
Sometimes you have to improvise

Sunset in Panarico

Brothers' tales from Panarico
(2014)

COCO FRIO O CALIENTE

We found this on the beach in Panarico
Where it came from someone knows
The claim was it was food and drink
That is how the story goes

This started when the brothers each drink
The coconut's delectable milk so sweet
But why not eat lunch
By having the coconut meat

When you are hungry for lunch
And potential is on the sand
You abandon the search for tools
And turn to your bare hands

I personally was filled with doubt
As many a coconut I had seen
Had been stubborn and mean
And kept its meat from going out
As some of the legends tell about
The boys had done many a crunch
A labor of legend of panarican lore
As coconut meat was served for lunch

Fairy Tale
A tale from the isthmus

The tide goes in
the tide goes out
there is one Fairy Tale
I wish to talk about
a little boy from the tropics has
Big Dreams in mind

He wanted to be happy but not
leave his roots behind

It all began with the isthmus where
Sunrise is east or west
he always seemed to have help
to make his fortune best

It All Began near the canal
a small average boy indeed
but he started very slow
And optimism was his Creed

the family went to Georgia a
taste of the US to see
as luck would have it a Black
Widow let him be
he missed kindergarten
it might have sealed his fate
the time was checked
he was right place right date
he went to Puerto Rico
to see the ocean blue
little did he know
the island was a big clue

first lesson was a bully
to which I deferred his due.
However, he met my sister
who left him black and blue

he was to go to New Jersey
bronze medal his father won [5]
not all things are perfect
as a new life had just begun

he eventually grew smarter
and a little brighter

he loved sports and knowledge
but was not much of a fighter.

Finishing Middle School
he won the final award
much to his surprise
scholar-athlete was in store

High School even better
he competed very well
his exploits were almost Legend
of which some elders tell

One of these stories was he finished the
geometry book in in one quarter….
Independent study the school would so order

he was academically very gifted
he did well most of the time
Very wonderful.
But sometimes life does not rhyme.
Was I prepared? when
Life gave me lemon and not lime.

for the first time in ages the school swept every test

he got the crown for the Math champion

because on that day he was best

He had received some help when he needed to switch high Schools

Many thanks to the reverend

Who saw something special in him

So much that the reverend

Created a special award

For the most competitive academically

The school had ever seen

(He had just been to the Science Bowl primarily to be an expert on physics. As that day was winding down, the team needed a miracle to place. As luck would have it the final question was in chemistry. The chemistry expert on the team said they did not know. They looked over to this young man who was completing an answer which the team agreed to submit and yes, they won.)

back then good fortune continued

so much that MIT accepted him quick

but Lafayette came knocking

and he wouldn't pay a lick

BSEE in 3
Bell Laboratories it was for me
finally he would switch
to work for WE
He mentored an amazing employee
his bride she was to be
dreams came true for me

Many a fine tale
they made and continued
but not for this writ
The purpose of this writing
will become apparent in a bit

There are three boys.
They have had made us very proud indeed
They are making their own tales
which I look forward to read
Is this truly a fairy tale? Can it really be?
i had 25 years of Parkinson's
and more is what we want to see

The path was not straight or easy or predictable, but there was a path. There were many dead ends, pits, and the like, but mostly I followed the light…

A PLETHORA OF SUPPORT (paradox)
2020

Eyes like sapphire,
Smile like pearl
You were always there
As I gave the planet a whirl

I always look at you
With amazement and wonder
You taught me that life
Is about sustaining, not plunder

Por que tan alta
My mother would say
Es pluscuamperfecta
And that she will stay

The definition of luck
Like her there is no other
I could sail the seven seas
And not find another

Three new kings
They shine so bright.
Because facing darkness.
You gave them the light.

It's time to say.
As the poet dances round.
A better role model?
Could never be found.

A perfect journey.
I have almost had.
You at my side
Makes me Googleplex glad.

I will be with you
Until our stars bend
You are always will be
My jewel and best friend

Interstitial story - I go to college

Short Story

I made it I had the opportunity to go to college in the United States. I got there and was petrified and wondered what I was going to experience. Americans seem so much smarter than me, they were taller than me, a lot of them made fun of me, and you see the picture I am painting is not one that brings a lot about having the big DREAMS. However, on the little island of Puerto Rico I had dreamed it so I should try to make my dreams come true. What the oracle had not mentioned was many a time getting a dream to come true requires hard work and sacrifice and there are no guarantees. Instead of turning around and going back home I decided to try the hard classes and see what happened. After getting 100 on the first Chemistry exam, moving from the freshman class to the sophomore class and in general competing well with all the students there, I BEGAN to feel more comfortable and more optimistic about my chances. My first year I was inducted into both ETA KAPPA NU and TAU BETA PI. I felt I could breathe again I was more optimistic that I was going to make it the whole way. But when confronted with the unknown and the stress it can cause, sometimes you just have to believe in yourself and remember that you bring something to the table as well. I had been close to calling my mom and asking for a ticket back, but as luck would have it, I called her after I turned it around and continued my dreams. I had gotten to Point B. okay. What and where was Point C...

Welcome Logan
(2021)

Logan has arrived

A very welcome plus one on the day

My Humble advice both of you

Please be ready to twist the night away

I was impressed by the repertoire if many a dance move

You all will sleep better

If rhythm is in your groove

Welcome Logan to la familia

Such wonderful news I found

Enjoy your loving parents

They are the best around

Clemson rocks
(2016)

They rolled out the tide.
It looked like they were there to stay.
A man on the Clemson sideline said.
You must beat the best to go the whole way.

Last year Clemson lost albeit exciting.
The fans all did recover.
This year the plot was still tbd.
With a few seconds to uncover.

The tide rode out.
For the moment they walked
But the welcome geo frat chanted.
Whose rocks were these.
Clemson rocks! Clemson rocks!

A black mustang flying the paw.
On an Orange flag on that day
Answering the need

More power to Clemson
To fight harder indeed

The game was a classic.
Both teams fired through the ramps
We knew with just seconds to go.
We were the national champs!

Your little Kyle
First Christmas 2000
To my mom

Here is a little something
I got for you to wear
When you don these magic rocks
You will always know I'm there

I am but ten months old
and you taught me to walk
In a just a few more weeks
I will begin to talk

I have one request
as I turn but one
when you don these magic jewels
remember me as my life had just begun

You will always be my mama
as I will be your son

I will always treasure you
and love you on and on

I must sign off now
lest Daddy know it
He knows all about me
except that I'm a poet

But please remember
as you always make me smile
I am and will always be
your "little" son Kyle.

(Earrings for MOM)

60 Fun (2020) Kronos 60 Reflections

As I lived mas 60
It is truly a time of reflection
The halcyon days remembered
Full of memories and introspection

My mom would say
Stand up in any crowd
You are another one
That has really made me proud

Some of you joined us right by birth
Some you joined by marriage
I hope you enjoy your life riding on the kings+
Enchantment and mystery carriage

I am her number one fan
And as the PanaRican[6] poet
In the face of amorphic Time
Every day she must know it

The majority of my work is done
All I have left should be fun
I continue to fight PD
Hope to live to say I won

Multiple aliases
Yes, many I have got
They all refer to me
Yes, perish the thought

The generations ahead
Will live long and prosper
The best have arrived
The dream team is my roster

I have faced Miami's Vader
He ended as a friend
Proof that it is better to share
Than to fight till the end

They call me by many names

- Panarican poet
- Oracle of the deep South
- The machine
- Kings
- Mage
- Dad
- Papi
- Pops

But remember
When you think of me
My major purpose was quite simply
To help you to get
from point A to B (to C, and adelante)

What is in the box you might say
Secret compartments and panels impede the way

Ense no sepa parle le francés
Kozonom in Budapest

I have traveled more than enough
Someone else can do the rest

Don that cape
Become that hero
Anything that you do
Is much greater than zero

DAY

NIGHT

What about sisters

Hey Mr.
Yes you
I heard you had a sister
Or two

There is a lot to be said about sisters
What say you Mr.
It's kind of like a resistor
I hear they are measured in ohms
That is useful when they are together or alone
But learn from them you will
Especially when they're older

And bolder

You think I read about steaks in geology class
Like pyrite to rock they may pass

As family we have our moments
But some albeit all in jest

But adding things up.
The book club?? Was the best??

Very healthy for the time we've got

You were and continue to be the best
And that is no jest

I am proud that you are always my sisters

love Mister

29
(2016, 2023)

The tide goes in.
The tide goes out.
Let me tell you.
albeit briefly.
What is this all about?

You are like a fine wine.
But, At your peak all the time.
And like a cherry blossom.
Always in State of prime.

Speaking of numbers.
Three boys.
29 years.
A couple.
Many associations.
With numbers prime.
We are not Fibonacci.
But we are the basis
Of this rhyme.

Lafayette College.
Clemson University.
Purdue University.
University of Pennsylvania.
University of Maryland.
University of Pittsburgh
University of Florida
Penn State University

Education is prime.
But I ask you to trust
For me to succeed.
Your happiness.
It is a must.

We should.
Enjoy every day. Every sunrise.
Because precious is this star
We hit home runs.
Out of the park they are.
Love. James.

The Sign

I think of all the signs I've seen across the world there is one sign that keeps coming back to me and has the most meaning. And, possibly the most relevance. I was driving from San Juan to Ponce one day as I was visiting. Puerto Rico, and I was with my children when we saw the sign. Most of the signs on the highway were bilingual signs So that the average tourist would have a chance of understanding what was Being warned. I am no expert on the International Convention of signage, But I believe yellow is associated with caution. My sons Looked at the sign with disbelief and ask me dad "Is there really a possibility of

¡PRECAUCION!
ᴾOSIBILIDAD GANADᴼ
EN EL RODAJE

having cows and bulls on the roadway.?" And as I thought about it I'd experienced That very thing At least three times in my experiences in Puerto Rico. Twice the road was blocked by a bull who wasn't in a hurry to move which puts you in a precarious situation If specially if someone behind you approaching you at a very high speed. I was also in a situation where they were crossing a herd of cattle across one of the expressways which goes to the radio telescope. But through over analysis I was also be able to create a lesson in life from this side My takeaway to the children was be prepared. You never know what you're going to see or experience along the way. You may be cruising on the highway (or life) and running into something unexpected Is very possible. So, expect the unexpected. Be Prepared for what life throws in as many surprises. If we run into a few pools on the road or a herd of cattle on a highway, just about anything else can happen. A lot of conclusions from one little sign in a different language But I always tell my children, there are opportunities to learn even when you don't think that is the case. But get out the sparkling grape juice because I am celebrating Life and the opportunities ahead. You should as well. Every day is an opportunity! If you believe that it is a good one your chances are that much higher of having a good day!

At least, that is what I believe most of the time.

Sancocho

Epilogue
25 years ago, I heard the word "Parkinson's"

I have lived a good happy life.
I am very self-motivated.
I get energy from family and friends
I plan to have a quality life
And keep going strong

The sun still rises
After all these years
Keep your chin up
As hope reappears

I will keep trying
Of that you can be sure
I hope to be ready
When they find the cure

First Equation of Parkinson's

$$x = a_1y_1 + a_2y_2 + \ldots$$
where
$$\text{sum } a_1 + a_2 + \ldots + a_n = 1 \text{ in steady state which is not normal.*}$$

* more discussion later.

X= Your Body and Mind

A (n) = coefficient of effect of the disease

Y (n) = attribute affected

++++++++++

I leave with an example of a graph I use to keep track of the major affected attributes over time. I use several graphs, but these are all part of getting the most quality from what I got. We live "running clock" but that does not prevent us from influencing the outcomes. I said in a presentation," I relate to running clock with PPM (points per minute) or in life, what do I accomplish per unit of time. In short, use PANARICAN TIME!

Chart Title

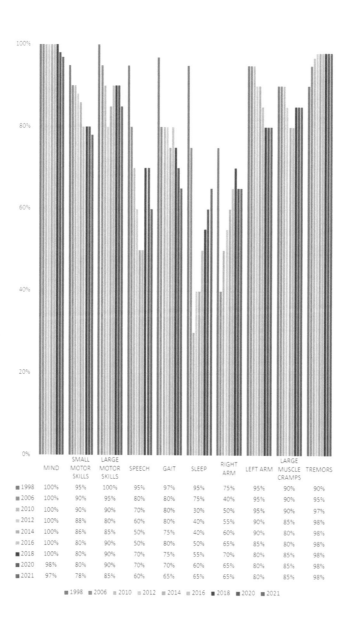

	MIND	SMALL MOTOR SKILLS	LARGE MOTOR SKILLS	SPEECH	GAIT	SLEEP	RIGHT ARM	LEFT ARM	LARGE MUSCLE CRAMPS	TREMORS
■ 1998	100%	95%	100%	95%	97%	95%	75%	95%	90%	90%
■ 2006	100%	90%	95%	80%	80%	75%	40%	95%	90%	95%
▨ 2010	100%	90%	90%	70%	80%	30%	50%	95%	90%	97%
▨ 2012	100%	88%	80%	60%	80%	40%	55%	90%	85%	98%
■ 2014	100%	86%	85%	50%	75%	40%	60%	90%	80%	98%
▨ 2016	100%	80%	90%	50%	80%	50%	65%	85%	80%	98%
■ 2018	100%	80%	90%	70%	75%	55%	70%	80%	85%	98%
■ 2020	98%	80%	90%	70%	70%	60%	65%	80%	85%	98%
■ 2021	97%	78%	85%	60%	65%	65%	65%	80%	85%	98%

■ 1998　■ 2006　▨ 2010　▨ 2012　■ 2014　▨ 2016　■ 2018　■ 2020　■ 2021

The Last Word

(2023)

If I had to conclude anything from the richness and vastness of all the experiences that I've had, and share words of wisdom, I'm not sure what I would say. There are some things I'm sure of. As I've had more experience with some things not going my way. I've been more careful to find out. What's the treasure? And if I know it's treasure. How do I keep it? Life is full of treasures. And it also has many paths that are dead ends and pits and holes to fall into.

As the clock never stops.
And continues to run.
Spend your time wisely.
And try to have fun.

Spend time with those you love. Make a difference where you can. We can all be better. Furthermore, with a little luck and effort, we will continue to add treasures and good memories to our treasure chest. There is a saying in Panarico, "If the box is too big. fill it with more worthy memories and treasures". I keep dreaming big and even now some of my biggest dreams have come true...but that my friend is another story...

Panarican Parrot

Endnotes

— • ● • —

1. Panarico – fictitious land created by the authors recognizing their parents' native homelands, Panama and Puerto Rico. All rights reserved.
2. Panarican Poetess – name created by author Judy as a descendent of Panarico. All rights reserved.
3. Panarican Poet – name created by author James as a descendent of Panarico. All rights reserved.
4. Pichicumba-family word created by authors' mom meaning "don't be cheap." All rights reserved.
5. Authors' father was a decorated war hero for his service in the Vietnam War.
6. PanaRican or Panarican – a native of Panarico. All rights reserved.

Printed in the United States
by Baker & Taylor Publisher Services